# VIKING

## BONUS CREATION

Viking Bonus Creation Page

# Chapter 1:
# Why Bonuses?

## Vendor Bonuses

If you are a product vendor, then you probably already know why you need bonuses. Bonuses are an excellent way to increase the perceived value of your product or offer. They also can significantly increase your conversion rates. Many of your buyers, no matter how good your product is, are sitting on the fence waiting for one last nudge towards becoming a customer. Bonuses can often be this difference between a buyer and a page abandoner. Then there are also those people who absolutely love the bonuses for the bonuses' sake and will actually judge your product based on the number of bonuses. So, making sure you have a good amount of attractive bonuses can go a long way towards maximizing your sales.

Finally, there is another, much less talked about, advantage of bonuses. They act as an excellent form of "collateral" that you can offer in your guarantee statement. Very few sellers do this, but it is incredibly effective and maximizes the amount of trust you can gain with potential buyers. Basically, what you do is you offer your standard guarantee, such as a 30-day money back guarantee, but then you state that you are going to "go above and beyond" and "reverse the risk". In this second part of your guarantee you are going to promise that the buyers, upon requesting a refund, will even get to keep the bonuses. If you have appraised the dollar value of these bonuses at, for example, $500, then you can pitch it as a "100% money back PLUS $500 value back guarantee". You might be asking "won't that just encourage people to buy with the full intention of requesting a refund just to get the bonuses for free?" The answer is YES. But, more importantly, the amount of people who will now buy the product, and otherwise would not have, far outweighs the number of "professional refunders" you will attract.

## Affiliate Bonuses

You may be asking yourself, why should affiliates bother with bonuses at all? Isn't that the vendor's responsibility?

Well, that might make sense if you want to be on the same even ground as all the other affiliates competing to make the sale with their affiliate link. But is that really what you want? Of course not! You want to be way out in the front. And it's been proven that offering bonuses as an affiliate can 5X your affiliate sales.

You need to give your audience a reason to use YOUR affiliate link instead of somebody else's. This is especially the case these days when people's inboxes are full of dozens of marketers pitching the same product to them. What is there to set you apart from the rest? Bonuses. That's literally it. Unless the buyer is your best buddy, all they really care about is which option gives them the most value. And rightfully so!

So the way this works is you create a quick and easy landing page, add bonuses to it and right at the top you tell them, grab all the bonuses on this page when you purchase "product x" via my link.

But you can't just slap a bunch of bonuses on that page and expect them to buy through your link. You've got to do it in a way that makes sense in relation to the product you're promoting and that is what we'll be covering next.

# Chapter 2:

# Keys to a Good Bonus

As mentioned previously, when you're offering bonuses as an affiliate you can't just do so with no rhyme or reason. The same goes for offering bonuses as a vendor. There has got to be some context and logical sense to the bonuses. Specifically, they need to have relevance, utility, and value. Not one or two of those. All three. Let's take a closer look at each of those.

## Relevance

You have to keep in mind you're dealing with real, intelligent human beings here. When a buyer is considering a product, the buyer is aware of the category and type of product and their thoughts are aligned with a specific "sphere". If the product is a list building product, they're mentally in the sphere of list building or lead generation. If you slap a bonus down that is way outside of that sphere, like a course on product creation, they'll notice a lack of relevance and they'll likely dismiss what you're offering. In fact, they might think you're just plain dumb.

On the other hand, if you offer them bonuses like landing page editors or a course on increasing their opt-in rate or a pack of lead magnets to use for list building, they'll immediately recognize that as something relevant to the list building product.

If necessary, you can stretch or "force" relevance for a category that is just "one step removed" from the category of the product. An example of this would be, "hey after you start building your list, you'll need to start marketing to them, so here's a course on email marketing". With that statement, you've established relevance. It's indirect, but it's only removed from the product category by one logical step. Buyers will notice the truthfulness of that relevance claim and it'll likely jive with them. If you try to go to many steps away from that original product category though, like "if you build a list you'll need email marketing (1 step) and if you do email marketing you'll need to do product creation to sell them something (2 steps)," then you'll create a logical disconnect and your bonus will seem irrelevant (because it is).

## Utility

Once you've satisfied the relevance requirement, you'll need to ensure your bonus has utility, or the ability to be utilized. Luckily, this is relatively easy because it goes hand in hand with relevance most of the time. The most effective type of utility, when it comes to bonuses, is augmentation. You want to present something that isn't just technically "useful" on paper, but something that specifically augments the intended purpose of the original product you're promoting. In this case, the more specific the usefulness, the better. For example, if the product is a course on list building, then simply handing over yet another course on general list building doesn't provide a specific type of usefulness. It's relevant, yes. And it's also "technically" useful, yeah. But it's not useful in a meaningful or specific way. Honestly, you could probably still get away with it, but the more specific the usefulness is, the more attractive the bonus will be and the more likely you are to get the commission for that sale. So, if the product was a list building course, then an exit intent WordPress plugin that presents a lead magnet and opt-in form as people try to leave your page would be a winner. It's relevant and useful, but it has specific usefulness, not just general, "technical" usefulness.

## Value

Once you know your bonus provides both relevance and utility, you need to ensure it provides value, both real and perceived. A potential buyer might look at your above-mentioned exit intent plugin and acknowledge that it has relevance and utility, but if it looks like it was created in 2007, they won't be too excited about it. This one is probably the most common problem you'll notice with bonuses put out by both vendors and affiliates. They all come from PLR or MRR wholesaler websites and usually only costed between $4 or $10 for a license. The problem isn't where they come from. The problem is that they still LOOK like they came from there. It doesn't matter if that eBook or course or plugin genuinely has value. If it lacks PERCIEVED value because it looks old and ugly as dirt, the buyer won't like it. We'll deal more with the "look and feel" of bonuses in chapter 4, but for now just be aware that looks play an important role in value. Furthermore, quantity and size are also major factors in value. A long eBook will seem more valuable than a "report", a multi-lesson video course will seem more valuable than a single video, and so on. That applies within each individual bonus but also to your collection of bonuses as a whole. Finally, rarity or uniqueness is important. By this we mean any bonuses that break the typical "eBooks and video courses" mold. This can include software tools, DFY landing pages, recorded interviews, advertising or traffic packages, consultations or strategy sessions, landing page critiques, and so on.

Now that you've got an idea of how to satisfy the big three requirements for a bonus, we'll need to figure out how to acquire them. And that's what we'll cover next.

# Chapter 3:
# Where to Curate Bonuses

## PLR or MRR Licensed Material

There are several ways and places to curate the materials you'll be using as bonuses. Probably the most common form of bonus material for affiliates, and for vendors who are just starting out, is PLR or MRR content. Basically, you acquire the rights to redistribute a product yourself and offer it as a bonus. There are two major ways to go about doing this. Buying newer PLR products that recently launched in a marketplace like JVZoo or WarriorPlus, or acquiring older materials from a PLR or MRR wholesaler.

The benefits of grabbing a recently-launched PLR product are pretty obvious. They're usually more attractive-looking and the material inside of them is usually more up-to-date. The downside, though, is that they're usually more expensive. This probably isn't a problem in the case of wanting just one or two bonuses. But if you're looking to maximize your conversions with a good stack of bonuses, this can be a serious issue, especially if you're just starting out and don't have much capital to spend.

The obvious benefit of approaching a wholesale PLR or MRR store (just google MRR store or PLR store) is that you'll be able to acquire several products for an incredibly low amount. The downside is that they will look old and may have out-of-date content. As long as it's not too severely out-of-date, this might not be a huge issue. Remember, you're giving this away for free, after all. But it is the old "look and feel" of the product that will result in a lower perceived value. Chapter 4 covers how to rectify this problem and re-package your bonuses in an attractive way (assuming that the license for your products included a right to modify the e-covers). Needless to say, you should always review these materials and ensure that they meet a minimum standard of quality and that their oldness is not so severe that they might harm your buyers' businesses.

## Using Your Own Materials

If you've been online for a while, there is a good chance that you'll already have existing content of your own. This might be blog content, lead magnets or reports you created, or even a collection of paid products of yours such as eBooks, video courses, or software. In the case of blog content, you would simply have to re-purpose this and re-package it as a bonus product (probably in eBook form). But in the case of existing products of your own, they might already be ready to go as-is. Worst case scenario, if they are a bit old, you'll want to create an updated e-cover for them.

# Chapter 4:
# Making Bonuses Attractive

Whether you got your bonuses from a PLR wholesaler or from your own old content, there's a good chance it suffers from a very common disease that plagues even some of the most famous marketers' bonuses: ugliness.

Now that may have sounded a bit comical, but the effect it can have on your conversion rates is no joke. Ugly bonuses kill sales. Period. If you're going to leverage bonuses to increase sales, they need to be beautiful. Here's how you do that.

First, take note of all of the components included in a bonus. In the case of a PLR/MRR product, you'll have to actually do some digging around inside the zip file and all of its folders. Did you find a resource guide? Write it down. Four videos? A folder named "bonus audios" with audio versions of the videos? An eBook? Yep, write it all down.

Next, you'll want to find your mascot/theme for this bonus. Go to an inexpensive stock photo site like PhotoDune or Adobe Stock. Look for an image of a man or a woman with a brightly colored (but not pure white) background. Make sure this is not the cliché business suit-wearing moron you are used to seeing from products made in 2008. Have you ever met an online entrepreneur who wears a damn tie? Seriously. The ideal look we're going for is the clean, casual entrepreneur with, for example, a button up shirt/blouse, collar opened, sleeves rolled up. The down to earth, rugged self-starter. That is the modern image of an entrepreneur that will resonate with your audience today.

Take that image and go to a site called myecovermaker.com (and yes, fork over the measly $14 for a full account). Go into the e-cover creator, choose one of the iMac-looking monitors, and upload your stock image. Zoom, crop, and arrange the model so he or she is a little off center and choose a dark font/text effect and write the title of the product. Once you've finalized that image and gone back to your dashboard, click edit on that same e-cover (which will create a duplicate), then change the template to a DVD case. You'll have to stretch and drag and rearrange the image and text to fit the new shape. Then, finalize and repeat this process with an audio cd case, a disk, eBook, etc. until you have a representation of each of those components you wrote down earlier. Download them all as transparencies.

Now it's back to the stock photo site again, this time to grab a background image. You're looking for a table top of some sort with a blurred background. Download this and open your favorite graphics program (Gimp is free and effective). Import those transparent e-cover images and arrange them with the iMac at the back and the other components in front of/on either side of it. Duplicate the various items to match the number of them in the bonus (e.g. four DVD cases if there are four videos, etc.).

What you should have is a gorgeous, sleek, new-looking image of the previously vomit-inducing bonus product. This will likely be one of most attractive bonus images your buyers have ever seen since almost no one else goes through the trouble of making their bonuses look good.

Now that you've got the gist of things, make sure you take action on what you've learned today and implement the following battle plan!

# Battle Plan

Step 1: Determine where you'll be curating your bonus content.

Step 2: Select bonus content that meets the three big criteria: relevance, utility, and value.

Step 3: Review the inside of your bonus content to ensure it meets minimum quality standards.

Step 4: Use the instructions above to produce a gorgeous representation of your bonus materials.

www.ingramcontent.com/pod-product-compliance
Lightning Source LLC
Chambersburg PA
CBHW071446210326
41597CB00020B/3953